Reaching the Pinnacle of Your Emotions

Vincent Carotenuto

Reaching the Pinnacle of Your Emotions

Copyright ©2009 by Vincent Carotenuto

All rights reserved by the author. No part of this publication may be reproduced, stored in a retrieval system or transmitted in any form or by any means electronic, mechanical, photocopying, recording or otherwise, without the prior written permission of the author.

ISBN: 978-0-578-03517-8

Library of Congress Control Number: 2009932613

Limit of Liability/Disclaimer of Warranty: While the author has used his best efforts in preparing this book for distribution, he makes no representations or warranties with respect to the accuracy of the contents of this book and disclaims any warranties of any purpose. The material and advice included in this book may or may not be suitable for your situation. You may wish to seek professional help where applicable.

This edition published by Vincent Carotenuto

To purchase additional copies, visit:

http://stores.lulu.com/vincentcarotenuto

Available at other fine retailers worldwide

Published in the United States of America.

Manufactured in the United States of America

CONTENTS

Disclaimer v

Acknowledgments vii

Read This First 1

Introduction 3

Chapter 1: Bad News 6

Chapter 2: Emotions... 10

Chapter 3: The Loops of Emotions 33

Chapter 4: The Extreme Emotion Questionnaires 39

Chapter 5: The Debate 46

Chapter 6: Perspective.. 50

Chapter 7: Visualization... 53

Chapter 8: In Closing 55

Frequently Asked Questions 57

Bonus – Key to Emotional Uplifting 63

A portion of the author's royalties on the sale of this book will be donated to The American Cancer Society.

DISCLAIMER

Although the contents of this book are most likely to help people, people may misinterpret the information provided and may cause hardship for some individuals. This is the reason for this disclaimer page. Always seek help from a certified professional if emotional stress becomes too great for you to handle alone. This book is written with the greatest good in mind. It is my firm belief that the human mind can change itself by changing the way we think and act. I want to note I am not a doctor, and nor do I have a degree of any kind. This book is intended for educational purposes only and is not intended to replace any professional advice you may have received. However, I truly believe this book will elevate your mood and help you understand why you feel the way you feel.

– Vincent Carotenuto

ACKNOWLEDGMENTS

If I were to list every person that has had a positive influence on me, the list would go on for pages and pages. I want to only mention a few names who I feel have had the most impact on me and who have helped me get where I am now: God, my family, John Murtha, Joseph Hart, co-workers and teachers. I would like to thank Code Nutrition customized vitamin supplements for the financial support they have provided to make this book possible. I cannot name everyone who helped me with making me who I am, but they know who they are, and I thank them.

READ THIS FIRST

"Another word for judgment is misunderstanding"

– Vincent Carotenuto

Thank you for picking up a copy of *Reaching the Pinnacle of Your Emotions*. This book is unlike any book you have ever read before. First of all, I am a nineteen-year-old high school graduate. I did not graduate high school with straight A's and a scholarship to college. I do not have any degrees that you may expect an author of a book about mental health to have. Monetary compensation was not a factor while making this book; any profit will help me pay for my college education and go to charitable causes. I was inspired to write this book because I want to help you, the reader, understand your emotions, as well as what causes them and what you can do in the very moment of experiencing the emotion to either elevate the pain you are experiencing, or prolong the joy you are feeling. Face it, we all want to be happy no matter what we are doing. You want to own a company? Why? Because you want to feel like you are in power? Why? So you can prove yourself to the world? Why? So you can show everyone who doubted you your worth? Why? So you can be happy, that's why! Everything comes back to one truth – we all want to be happy. I am writing this book because I want to be happy! I will be happy if people benefit from this material and use it in their daily lives.

I hope you will not discredit this information I have provided for you because I do not have a title next to my name. I hope this mere fact has encouraged you to see things from a different perspective. If you have not purchased this book yet, I encourage you to do so. Just one piece of information in this book could very well change the way you think, and ultimately change the way you live your daily life. After reading this book, you may be able to look right at a negative situation, take a moment to review the material in this book, and come out of the situation relieved that you stayed calm and controlled the situation instead of having the situation control you. My friends, I believe most people will benefit from this book. So let's begin this unique journey and let's learn about our emotions and how to control them easily.

Yours truly,

Vincent Carotenuto

INTRODUCTION

"In your worst mood, your best one grows"

– Vincent Carotenuto

I want to start this book by asking you, the intelligent reader, a question. I know you are intelligent because you are reading this book, which tells me that you are smart enough to know that your emotions affect every aspect of your life. You realize that you may discover important information that can enhance the quality of your life. My question to you is: how are you feeling at this very moment? Are you feeling depressed? Are you in a negative mood right now? You are, you say? Put this book down. Do not read any further at the current time. I need you to go and pursue an activity that you enjoy; I don't care what it is, as long as it is legal of course. I need you to be in a positive state of mind while reading this book. The reason for this is because when people are in a low mood and go about their activities, they are not really fully benefiting from the experience. They are not paying attention to it, absorbing the information, and learning from what they are doing. So I ask you to only read this book when you are in a higher state of emotion if you want to truly appreciate and benefit from the book.

When I first started writing this book, I didn't even know how to describe the book. I started out saying it is an emotion dictionary. Then I thought about it and wanted my readers to get more bang for their buck, so I added some concepts and diagrams for you to understand things a little bit more clearly. I added quotes for inspiration to keep your brain working and keep you thinking positive, which is *crucial* for success, and I will explain this in greater detail later in this book. I have added some other things to make this book enjoyable and memorable for you because I don't know about you, but I get frustrated when I purchase a book and forget some of the important concepts in the book! I kept this in mind when I wrote the book because I care about my readers. So you can expect to find ways to make your mental health a little bit easier to understand and improve upon.

Reaching the Pinnacle of Your Emotions is a universal book. No matter who you are, you can benefit from the content that is in front of you. I also didn't want to write a long book because I don't want your attention span to dwindle and you not fully comprehend the content. The more I write and the more ideas I throw at you, the less you will remember them and the chances of you misinterpreting this data increases.

Your emotions are everything, do you understand this? Yet most people go through life trying to just get by day by day and hoping the next day will get better. They figure life has to be like this, and they can't help it that other people ruin their day. You really control your own life, other people may impact your life, but you are in the driver's seat, my friend. What it boils down to is that you make yourself feel however you want to feel! You do this, not your miserly boss! Everything is influenced by how you are feeling, from the music you listened to on the way to work to the warm greeting you offered the new associate at the office.

Emotions are something many people do not pay attention to, people think they come and go, and there is no system to how we feel and no way to prevent or prolong any feeling we may face. Yet I tell you this, my friends, with a little bit of practice we can control our emotions. You can feel a sense of ease in a moment of uncertainty, disregard a negative conversation you overheard in work, elongate the feeling of pure bliss and love, and this book will show you how. Follow me, my friends.

Chapter 1

Bad News

"All that we are is the result of what we have thought. The mind is everything. What we think we become."

– Buddha

I have some bad news for you. This book will not eliminate every negative emotion you will experience. I don't want you to go into this book thinking you will become happy and never experience negative emotions in your life. I believe that is impossible, but if you know how to do that, please e-mail me right away! You see, many people are on an emotional roller coaster. We experience new emotions all the time; many of us experience at least two or more different emotions per hour.

If you really think about that statement, you can see how that rings true. Think about when you are at work, your emotions generally change very often. We need to have some negative emotions in our lives so we can appreciate and understand positive emotions that happen to us. Without experiencing the negative, we would not appreciate the positive. So when a negative event happens to you, know that a positive event is right around the corner.

So now that you understand that this book (or any book) will not bring you joy every moment of every day, allow me to explain what this book will provide for you. *Reaching the Pinnacle of Your Emotions* will give you the information you need to get through your day armed with knowledge, self-esteem, and inspiration to improve your emotional well-being. This book will give you a different way to think. You may have a hard time changing the way you think at first, but with a little bit of constant positive thought, you will notice that you are thinking in a different way, and as time passes, this will become your dominate way of thinking.

If you start to go back to your old, habitual way of thinking, that is fine. Just recognize what triggered this and make a mental note that you will not do this again. Tell yourself, "I'm not going to let Mike at work ruin the way I feel any longer, he no longer has power over me and will not impede my chances of a promotion." If that statement holds true for you, you will, with a little bit of practice, mostly likely realize that Mike really doesn't bother you as much as he did before. Try this activity if you do not believe me.

You do, however, have to say to yourself in a good amount of detail what it is that you want. You can't just say, "He is not going to bother me any longer." You have to give some details and make this statement stick out to you so the next time you encounter this situation, you remember what you promised yourself. This is an activity I use on an ongoing basis and the results are surprisingly pleasant. This statement becomes more real to you if you do it yourself instead of your friends just telling you, "Don't worry about that." You may shrug this off and think they are just saying that because they are not in your situation. Try it next time, I think you will change around some circumstances to make your statement true for you.

Here is another activity you can do that will make your day go great! When you feel happy in the daytime (the earlier the better), prolong this feeling as much as possible. Do not allow anything to upset you because if you stay positive and happy, your day will go in that general direction. This happens every time, even if you are not aware of this. We have all heard the saying, "This day keeps getting worse and worse," well, that is true if your dominant thought is negative, your day will be negative for you. Here is what I do to reap the benefits of this; I sometimes trick my mind to pretend everything is fine even if I am extremely angry. You really can trick yourself and gain the positive results of this mind experiment! Unfortunately, sometimes just feeling sad for a few minutes can very well ruin the positive results.

My friends, if you enhance your emotional health, you have the power to change everything in your life. Nothing seems too big for you to conquer when you are in a positive emotional state, know that with a little bit of practice, you can acquire a positive emotional state for the majority of your life!

Perspective is such a big thing that I have devoted a full chapter to it just so you can better understand how your perspective changes everything about a situation. Perspective can change the way you think about something in such a radical way; it is fascinating to see things from a different angle. I firmly believe that your inner world shapes your outer world. If this theory holds true, you become unstoppable! You have the power to do anything you want to do because you live with a balanced, healthy, emotional state of mind.

We are supposed to be happy in life, that is the way life is meant to be. Many of us go against life instead of going with it. We tend to make things what they are not, we blow up and exacerbate our problems to the point that our day is ruined every time we think or talk about them. Based on my findings, most people become happy when we go with the flow of life and eliminate worries as much as possible. This is so much easier said than done, but once you change the way you think, your brain tends to rewire and think differently.

I remember a few years ago, I was having a conversation with a coworker and I asked her, "How do you always stay so happy? Every time I see you, you're happy, what's your secret?" Her response made me really think, even to this day, years later. She answered, "It's easy, I just don't think of bad things." I pondered this statement over and over and concluded that this is great advice. It is important to note that whenever we are in a negative situation, we must learn to change the thought as quickly as possible, the sooner the better actually. I believe this book will become an asset to your emotional health. As with anything else, it will help you if you seek out information from other sources because, as we all know, knowledge is power. It is my strong belief that when you have finished this book, you will realize that you are truly on your way to reaching the pinnacle of your emotions!

Chapter 2

Emotions

"Feelings will pass with the daylight, but they will leave a trail for which future ones will follow."

— Vincent Carotenuto

Do you know that your emotions can make you ill? More and more conclusive research indicates that the way you feel can cause disease. The way you think can also reverse disease! Your emotions are always tied into how you are thinking, and how you are thinking makes a big difference in your overall state of being.

Some of the information presented in this book may seem like basic information for the most part, I discourage you from skipping over this. When you are experiencing a particular emotion, read the information provided and learn more about your emotion to either prolong the joy, shorten the pain, or appreciate the state of being you are currently experiencing. You can also read the book to gain knowledge so you can put the advice in action as soon as you feel a particular emotion. There is no wrong way to read and benefit from this book. When you learn more about an emotion, the next time you notice yourself entering into that emotion, think of the information presented here and you can choose to proceed with this emotion or choose another one.

Our brains remember events that occurred in the past. Based on that information, we conclude if a situation will leave us in a negative mood or a positive mood. I find it interesting that a lot of times we feel bad is because of past experiences. Sometimes there is nothing that is occurring to you right now for you to feel bad at all except your own thoughts about the past repeating over again.

What would you say if I told you that you could choose your emotions? Well, I am telling you that indeed you can choose your own emotions, and we do it every time we have an emotion. You are choosing to cry when you are sad. You have one hundred percent freewill to feel however you want to feel in any circumstance. You may say it is natural to feel bad if you lose your job. Of course, you would say that would be your normal response, but you *choose* that. You could have felt positive that you will find an even better job, right? We all choose our emotions, and it is up to you to feel however you *want* to feel. It will, however, require practice and discipline at first, but, my friends, you can really control your emotions.

Once you learn to control your emotions, gates that were closed before open up. You are now able to view the situation in a different way, in doing this you allow yourself to also view solutions in a different way. The goal of this chapter is to recognize your emotion, possible reasons for your emotion, along with suggestions that may remedy your situation. I have also included important points to remember for each emotion mentioned as well as words of encouragement. This may help you when you feel like you are alone (in reality you are never alone), as well as help you get through rough times. I had the reader in mind when I produced this material, so I used an easy-to-read format which saves you time and allows you to remember information more easily. This is important because we are all busy and want quick answers.

You may think that the suggestions here are common sense and are commonly suggested, but I only listed the suggestions that I feel really work to help people get through an emotion with a happier state of emotion. You may also note some repetition with the causes and suggestions, but that is only because there are similar causes and remedies. Some of the information presented in this chapter may not even be categorized as an emotion, but I feel they are important to list nevertheless. Even if you read the suggestions and you believe you already knew them, try them! You may be really surprised that they will work for you, and they will help you in your time of distress or elongate your time of joy. Sometimes the simple, basic advice tends to be the most effective in yielding positive results.

I would like to note that not every emotion is listed here. Most common emotions and emotional states are however, which I believe will help the majority of readers. It is interesting to note that every emotion stems from either love or fear. If you experience a negative emotion that really bothers you, you will have a feeling of instant loss. If you see something that really upsets you, you feel loss in some way. Whether that feeling of loss is loss of control, possessions, current environment – all negative emotions lead to a feeling of loss. That is what bothers you, you are afraid you are or will lose something in some way.

The same principal applies with positive emotions. When you experience a strong positive emotion, you feel love in some way. Positive emotions lead to love, whether love of people, love of possessions, love of life – positive emotions are love. I call these two emotions 'Core Base Emotions' (CBE). Remember these emotions and choose love!

Anger

Emotion: Anger

CBE: Fear

Why you feel like this: Mental stress, physical stress.

What you could do: Relaxing exercises, listen to your favorite music (regardless of genre), go outside, sleep, confront your problem in a peaceful manner regardless of opposition, reminisce about past pleasant events, see the problem from a different viewpoint.

Important things to remember: Everyone gets angry at one point or another. If you are really angry right now, relax and think about what you are angry about and think if it will matter five years from now. No, you say? What if you act irrationally now, will your actions last longer than your temporary state of anger? Most likely. The best thing to remember when you are angry is that this will soon pass, and you will feel better as time passes. Keep your cool and ride out the storm.

Quote:

"He who angers you conquers you."

– Elizabeth Kenny

Acceptance

Emotion: Acceptance

CBE: Love

Why you feel like this: Positive social interaction with others, higher self-respect for oneself.

What you can do: Take a moment to realize your true worth, eliminate negative thoughts during this time period, participate in activities that you enjoy.

Important things to remember: When you feel accepted in something, no matter if it is an acceptance letter into a college, or you feel accepted in a group at work, you want to stay positive. You have the ability to ruin any situation by allowing negative thoughts into your mind. It may help you to prolong this experience by realizing that you deserve this feeling of acceptance. Due to your higher level of motivation, now may be a perfect time to accomplish activities that you may have otherwise delayed.

Quote:

"Give love and unconditional acceptance to those you encounter, and notice what happens."

– Wayne Dyer

Amusement

Emotion: Amusement

CBE: Love

Why you feel like this: External environment, internal environment.

What you could do: Elaborate on the situation in which you find amusing, incorporate others in this event to enhance the effect, remember how great you feel right now and think of this when you enter into a negative mood, continue to find more material for your amusement.

Important things to remember: Laughing feels so great and it is healthy for you! I am not pretending to be a doctor but your body has a pH of either alkaline or acidic. Disease is said to be less prevalent in an alkaline pH and laughter is one of the things that will turn your pH to alkaline! So remember that while you are having a good time laughing, you are helping your health out. One of the best things about being amused is many times you can revisit the situation in your mind and still laugh at it weeks, months, or even years later. Laugh as often and as much as you can because being amused is something that can make your day, even after many "bad" days.

Quote:

"Laughter is the shortest distance between two people."

–   Victor   Borges

Boredom

Emotion: Boredom

CBE: Fear

Why you feel like this: Lack of stimulating activities, lack of new information, repetition of actions or thoughts.

What you could do: Break a repetitive pattern, engage in activities that provoke humor, ponder quantum physics, read books, watch movies, enjoy Mother Nature, sleep, listen to music, think of how far you came from your past self to your present self.

Important things to remember: Think of this state of boredom as beneficial for your overall well-being. We all have times when we are so busy that we become depressed. We constantly multitask in order to get things done. When you are bored, you may have more than enough time. If you are bored because you are engaging in a mundane task, take heart to know that you are benefiting someone in some way. A great activity that you may enjoy is to envision the future of your dreams in great detail. Also, believe that it can happen and get excited about it. This gets you motivated and often relieves your boredom. Sometimes being bored provides a much-needed break from the hectic fast-paced world we live in. Enjoy it.

Quote:

"If you're bored with life – you don't get up every morning with a burning desire to do things – you don't have enough goals."

– Lou Holtz

Disappointment

Emotion: Disappointment

CBE: Fear

Why you feel like this: Past negative experiences arise, over-projecting results, allowing the external world to have more control than the inner world.

What you could do: No longer expect something to happen based on a past result, realize things are just that, things. Stay positive and realize that better things will occur.

Important things to remember: Disappointments always make us really blue. We like things to go smoothly just as expected without a hurdle on the track. Things don't always go that smoothly of course. The key to not being disappointed is not to discontinue wanting things, just do not place as much importance in them if you do not get them. Want it, get excited about it, but do not get on the level that you will be sad if you do not receive it. Always keep in mind that you will receive something even better if you just have faith and patience.

Quote:

> **"One's best successes come after their greatest disappointments."**
>
> – Henry Ward Beecher

Depression

Emotion: Depression

CBE: Fear

Why you feel like this: Imbalanced state of mind, negative dominate thoughts, no or few goals for the future, physical ailments, low self-esteem, death of loved one, illness, financial matters, playing the role of a victim.

What you could do: Participate in your favorite healthy activities whatever they may be, exercise, read inspirational books, look to a positive role model, talk to friends, seek help from a professional if appropriate, take a step to achieve a goal of yours or perhaps make new goals, think positive and dream big, write a book or invent a product or idea, enter free contests, pray.

Important things to remember: Depression is one of the emotions that in my opinion is the most detrimental to your health, well-being, and loved ones. First, you being depressed is not your fault, and you are meant to experience this in your life for some reason you may very well find out in the future. You must not give up hope, and you must stay positive no matter what comes your way. You may want to seek professional help if you feel you cannot handle this amount of depression. I discovered that many times mild forms of depression can be alleviated by breaking the current pattern of life. Start something new that you enjoy. Financial hardships and death are other major contributors to depression and should not be handled alone. You should always seek help from loved ones and professionals if you feel you are extremely depressed. Medicines may help those suffering from depression also. Self-help and religious books may also help out those in need of extra support and comfort.

Quote:

"Depression is anger without enthusiasm."

– Anon

Embarrassment

Emotion: Embarrassment

CBE: Fear

Why you feel like this: Humiliating external or internal event.

What you could do: Learn to focus more attention on your inner world rather than the external world, realize we are not infallible, if the occurrence is insignificant, you should allow the event to go by with time and not place any attention on the embarrassing situation, rationalize the situation to others, make a joke about it.

Important things to remember: Embarrassment is something that happens to all of us and can actually keep us on our toes and keep us alert to what is going on around us. When we become very embarrassed, we tend to remember the situation for quite some time. This can be good or bad depending on how you look at it. It can be good because this event has put a mental note in your brain allowing you to alter your behavior in the future so this doesn't happen again. It can also be a bad thing because you can develop a phobia if you do not allow this to pass and not give any attention to the incident. The best thing you can do if the situation is small is just to let it pass or make a joke about it because humor cures numerous negative emotions.

Quote:

"If you are never scared, embarrassed or hurt, it means you never take chances."

– Julia Soul

Energetic

Emotion: Energetic

CBE: Love

Why you feel like this: Artificial or natural energy enhancing substances, feeling the joy of life, well-rested, in a natural emotional state, full of hope and desires.

What you could do: Stay in this state as long as you can, as you will accomplish much and have fun doing it, remember what caused you to become like this so you can replicate this in the future, realize that this is how life can be for you if you take control of your health and emotional state, accomplish tasks you otherwise would put off, exercise.

Important things to remember: This is the way your life is supposed to feel. Notice how good you feel when you are bursting with energy! You feel like you can't be stopped by anyone. You feel like you can solve the world's problems! This is a great emotion to have and you can accomplish many things when you are in this state. It may help you if you actually talk yourself into having energy even when you feel as if you are running out of energy to elongate this great feeling! This will usually work when you are in such a high frequency, as you will have the imagery to really change your brain and reinstate the fact that you are full of lasting energy!

Quote:

"Energy and persistence conquer all things."

– Benjamin Franklin

Fear

Emotion: Fear

CBE: Fear

Why you feel like this: Lack of solid faith in oneself or in a higher being, imagination programmed to think of the worst possible case, you feel unworthy and alone, afraid of ridicule, afraid of present environment change, you feel inferior to others, pain, isolation, death, the unknown, numerous other emotional and physical causes.

What you could do: Fear not as fear disappears once you look at it directly and see that you will prevail. Facing your fear is the only way in my opinion to dissolve fear.

Important things to remember: Fear is what stops millions of people from inventing that million-dollar invention. Fear is what causes you to decline that promotion or to succumb to your unfair supervisor. Fear paralyzes you and your dreams. I believe the only way to get over your fear permanently is to confront it and confront it in different situations and different times. If you are afraid of making a big speech and you finally make it and you do great, are you no longer afraid of speaking? Most likely not as in a few months you may be in the same situation. I believe you must face your fear announced and unannounced and in different situations in order to really overcome it. But my friends, you will feel great after you finally get over your fear or phobia.

Quote:

"Do the thing you fear to do and keep on doing it… that is the quickest and surest way ever yet discovered to conquer fear."

– Dale Carnegie

Joy

Emotion: Joy

CBE: Love

Why you feel like this: Past negative circumstances lifted, perspective changed, positive circumstances presently felt.

What you could do: Participate in activities that make you feel good to maintain this feeling, eliminate all negative thoughts the moment you think of them, listen to music, avoid negative people at all costs.

Important things to remember: You want to stay in the state as long as possible; this is why positive thoughts are vital. However, some may think so positively that they actually start doubting what they are thinking! So you start out positive, you add more positive thoughts thinking that this will just make you that much happier, and you actually sabotage yourself! If you enjoy taking a hot shower, do that! If you enjoy taking a nap, do that! Whatever it takes for you to stay happy and peaceful, it is in your best interest to do. Remember, when you are in the state of joy, you can accomplish anything.

Quote:

"Joy is not in things; it is in us."

– Richard Wagner

Jealousy

Emotion: Jealousy

CBE: Fear

Why you feel like this: Personal insecurity of one's self image, lack of understanding, feeling of betrayal, feeling of greed, anger.

What you could do: Look at life from a different perspective, realize that you are not meant to have this particular thing you are jealous of at this time, show love, become grateful for your own possessions, realize that no one has everything.

Important things to remember: Jealousy is something that can become very powerful. Jealousy can also become a good motivator to obtain the things you want to have. You must never reach a level where personal possessions mean everything to you. It may help to realize that if someone is living richly while you are in a challenging financial situation, that person may not have someone that loves them while you do. Keep things in perspective and watch jealousy disappear.

Quote:

"To cure jealousy is to see it for what it is, a dissatisfaction with self."

– Joan Didion

Love

Emotion: Love

CBE: Love

Why you feel like this: Alignment with your natural emotion, which is love, material possessions, feelings of respect, viewing life in a different perspective, disappearance of a physical or mental obstacle, change, positive emotions.

What you could do: Do activities that you enjoy, stay in a positive state, savor all happy moments in your life and replay them in your head, remember the fact that we all are equal and no one is superior, let the small things go, play music as often as you like, spend time with funny people.

Important things to remember: Love is the ultimate emotion – the king of feelings. It is the emotion that we try to reach by every action we take in this world. We all want to be loved so we can give love back. We were born with love, each and every one of us. When you are in a loving mood, I urge you to only come into contact with people that will enhance your feeling of love. Try to avoid people who zap you from feeling love. Every action we take in this world is linked back to the bottom line, which is we want to be loved. When you feel loved, you are in a euphoric state. Receive love, but give it back to others as often as possible.

Quote:

"Love builds bridges where there are none."

– R.H Delaney

Loneliness

Emotion: Loneliness

CBE: Fear

Why you feel like this: Lack of positive human intervention, misconception that one is alone in their troubles.

What you could do: Interact with people who share your troubles, research your problem, realize you always have someone watching over you, listen to music, read spiritual books, watch humorous movies or television shows, take your mind of the problem to alleviate the constant stress.

Important things to remember: I believe that if you are feeling lonely, you may benefit from reading a self-help book. This will give you encouragement and make you become positive, which may help get you out of the negative emotion of loneliness. Loneliness is a powerful emotion that stems from fear. We all have an innate desire to be around others who love us; I believe that is why loneliness is a very serious emotion that can really cause us to lose focus of what is important in life. If you are feeling lonely, remember you are only alone in your own mind, not in reality.

Quote:

"The eternal quest of the individual human being is to shatter his loneliness."

– Norman Cousins

Optimism

Emotion: Optimism

CBE: Love

Why you feel like this: Positive events that occurred or are occurring in your life, embraced by self-love or by others' love, faith that everything will work out fine in the end, material possessions.

What you could do: Meditate, read your favorite book, associate with good friends, relax, stay positive, do not allow anyone to make you think what you are optimistic about will not work out.

Important things to remember: Stay in this positive state and you will notice how other positive emotions come to you, such as love and joy. It is important to have unwavering faith that you will have success in your life and achieve anything you put your mind to. It is important to ignore anyone who tries to break your optimistic state of mind. They may not do it intentionally, but they will do it if you are not careful. You may not think optimism is an emotion per se, but it is something that I believe is worth being included in the book's emotions reference pages.

Quote:

"Optimist: A man who gets treed by a lion but enjoys the scenery."

– Walter Winchell

Peacefulness

Emotion: Peacefulness

CBE: Love

Why you feel like this: You allowed harmony into your life, you realize we are all one, you are filled with love.

What you could do: Maintain this feeling of being at ease by enjoying pleasant activities, ignoring disempowering thoughts, promise yourself to eliminate any grudges you may have with individuals, forgive everyone, try to realize everything people do is acceptable in the way they see things.

Important things to remember: If someone gets you angry, remember that there is a reason that they feel you may deserve this. The key to living peacefully is realizing that nobody wants to be a pain, or try to willingly cause pain or heartache for no reason. They see things differently, and if you come to realize that, you will live in peace with yourself and others.

Quote:

"Peace comes from within. Do not seek it without."

– Buddha

Pessimism

Emotion: Pessimism

CBE: Fear

What you could do: Do as little as possible in this state, realize everything will seem negative and that is an inaccurate observation, relax and sleep if you can, talk to good friends, watch funny videos or comedies, participate in leisure activities, do something different.

Why you feel like this: external causes such as people, environment, etc, inadequate sleeping time, overload of stress, repetition of daily tasks.

Important things to remember: Everything you do will most likely seem like a chore and something that you do not believe is worth it any longer. Realize this is an inaccurate observation and is biased because of your pessimistic mood. It may help you to do as little as possible when you are in this mental state because of this fact. If you would like to do activities still, it may help you to do something different to break the cycle of repetition. Sleep will help your mood along with humorous activities.

Quote:

"Dr. Miller says we are pessimistic because life seems like a very bad, very screwed-up film. If you ask 'What is wrong with the projector?' and go up to the control room, you find it's empty. You are the projectionist, and you should have been up there all the time."

– Colin Wilson

Surprised

Emotion: Surprised

CBE: Love *or* fear

Why you feel like this: Positive or negative unexpected internal or external events.

What you could do: go with the flow of the incident, appreciate if the event is positive or learn from the event if it is negative, keep positive, appreciate that surprise is the spice of life.

Important things to remember: Surprise is one of the only emotions that can bring complete joy or complete sorrow. It is important to go with the flow if the surprise is a minor inconvenience, and appreciate any small pleasant surprises. Think of how boring your life could be without any surprises – good or bad. Would you want to live your life every day knowing exactly what will happen, even if you can't change it? You may initially but when this becomes a pattern over time, this will irritate you more than you may think.

Quote:

"Surprise is the greatest gift which life can grant us."

– Boris Pasternak

Thoughtfulness

Emotion: Thoughtfulness

CBE: Love

Why you feel like this: Realization that love is what makes the world go around, you take joy out of helping others.

What you could do: Continue being thoughtful and helping out others, appreciate the things you have in your life, thus allowing you to give more to others, listen to music as music tends to mellow us and make us return to a caring mood.

Important things to remember: When you are being thoughtful, you allow the best of yourself to show to the world. Even something small can mean big things to people even if you never realize it. Once you start thinking of others before yourself, you start to get into the habit of doing so and you become a thoughtful, kind, considerate human being.

Quote:

"Never doubt that a small group of thoughtful, committed citizens can change the world; indeed, it's the only thing that ever does."

– Margaret Mead

Chapter 3

The Loops of Emotions

"The true test of emotional strength occurs when in immediate emotional distress."

— Vincent Carotenuto

Many a night, I would sit down and wonder if there was any system that we experience when we feel feelings. Over many months of carefully planning and evaluating information, I have created what I call the 'Loops of Emotions'. There are two loops which we follow, one for each mood set. The loops are the Higher Feeling Process Loop (HFPL) and Lower Feeling Process Loop (LFPL).

The HFPL includes five emotions that are all present when we are in a positive mood. The same principle applies with the LFPL. The purpose of the loops is to illustrate how emotions are connected and flow from one like emotion to the next. The loops can help you see how if you experience just one of the emotions in the loops, you are more likely to climb into the next emotion and the circle continues. This is great news when you are in the HFPL, but devastating when you are feeling an emotion in the LFPL.

I want you to realize how your emotions are connected and how one leads to the other. Every day I see people who allow their feelings to run on autopilot. They allow outside circumstances to determine how they are feeling in the current time. Many people think this is how *everyone* behaves, yet I tell you this, this is categorically false.

When you realize there is a pattern to your emotions, you will realize it is in your best interests to not even think twice about the small things that happen in our life that we allow to upset us. Quite the contrary, the loops will show you how once you are in a positive mood your mood will not change unless you find something negative to break the loop.

To me, there is nothing more encouraging than having a great day, free of major negative occurrences. If you have not had one in a while, you can claim tomorrow to be a great day. You can predict if tomorrow will be a good day for you by the thoughts you have felt when you read that. Those who will have a good day are feeling pumped, excited, motivated and have faith that they have more power than they are led to believe. Those who will have an average day are feeling like this is all wishful thinking and whatever happens will happen regardless of any influence from them. Which one of these people are you? Which one do you want to become?

Higher Feeling Process Loop

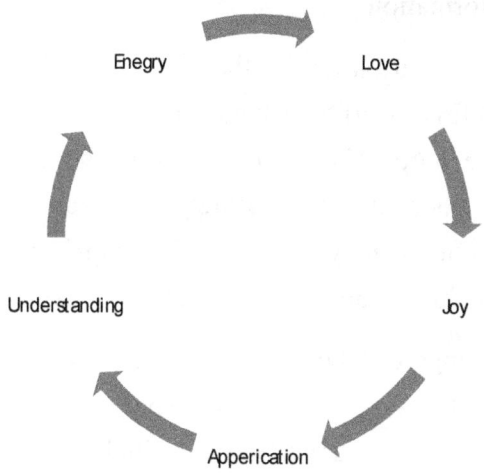

This is the HFPL. Love, Joy, Appreciation, Understanding and Energy make up this loop. You may wonder why energy is in this loop, but if you think about it, it is very simple. Have you ever seen someone who seems to have all these emotions and did not have any energy at all? Excluding any medical conditions, most likely not. As soon as you feel love, if you stay in this state long enough, you will find things that make you joyful. When you are feeling joyful, you tend to look around and appreciate things, people, and circumstances more. When we appreciate things, we need to understand why things are the way they are. When we are understanding of something, there is no negative feeling involved. Everything we do is appropriate and justifiable, given the way we see things happening in the world and our lives. If you remember that, you will save yourself a lot of stress and agitation. When we understand things, we get a natural rush of excitement and love which gives us energy. We want to know more, do more, see more and experience more now that we know new information.

If you keep on a particular thought, you will move through this loop indefinably. If you break the thought or feeling, you will break the loop. The amount of time it may take you to complete the loop depends entirely on each individual and circumstance. Some may complete the loop in minutes with a thought, others hours, others days, months, or even years.

Higher feelings can be simply classified as any feeling that makes one feel good. The next time you experience a higher feeling, stop what you are doing and think about how you are feeling now. Feel how good it feels to be alive and realize that no matter what else happens in your life, no matter how bad it seems at first, you will always go back to this state of higher feeling. This is not just positive thinking, this is true in every circumstance. Even if you do not think you are happy, are you happier now than you were in your past? If you still don't believe me that you will return to a higher feeling emotional state, just wait. You may not be ready to experience the positive circumstances that will happen to you just yet, but with patience you will return to a positive state.

Lower Feeling Process Loop

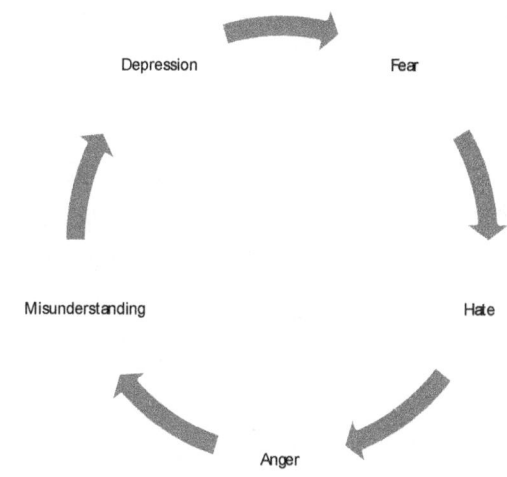

This is the LFPL. The Lower Feeling Process Loop consists of Fear, Hate, Anger, Misunderstanding and Depression. All of these feelings stem from Fear. Fear starts every negative emotion known to man. We hate because we are afraid, we feel anger because anger is fear disguised, when we are depressed, we are afraid. Misunderstanding is something that may have thrown you off-guard in the loop, but hear me out.

Whenever we argue, it is simply a lack of understanding. We simply do not see the other party's viewpoint. Sometimes it is that we do see it, just that we do not understand or the reason does not resonate with our beliefs. You may find that the loop of the LFPL is easier to understand and agree with since we all seem to follow this set of feelings rather than the HFPL's set of feelings.

It is important to realize that when you feel bad, it not only hurts you emotionally, but it also hurts you physically. Always try to offset each negative emotion by experiencing a positive emotion from the HFPL. When you are in the middle of the LFPL, you feel horrible. You feel like anything that anyone has ever told you that was positive was a lie.

When I am stuck in the LFPL, I always remember that whenever something negative happens, a positive experience always follows. It helps to keep things in perspective when the going gets tough. It is not just wishful thinking, it really is true and happens every time. It may also help you to realize that you would not enjoy the HFPL if you have not experienced the feelings in the LFPL. Rapper 50 Cent proved this by saying, "Sunny days wouldn't be special if it wasn't for rain, Joy wouldn't feel so good if it wasn't for pain." You need to experience contrasting emotions in order to really appreciate the good things in life.

Chapter 4

THE EXTREME EMOTION QUESTIONNAIRE

"He who envisions positive thoughts on a daily basis is predisposed to the wealth one is entitled to."

— Vincent Carotenuto

The Extreme Emotion Questionnaire is a questionnaire I have designed to assist you when you are experiencing an extreme emotion. There is one questionnaire for when you are experiencing a positive emotion, and one for when you are experiencing a negative emotion. I designed these questionnaires only for when you are feeling extreme emotions, you may not benefit from them as much as I would like you to if you use them at any given emotion.

If on a scale from 1-10, 10 being the most intense emotion you have ever experienced, you rate your present feeling anything over an 8, I would highly suggest you fill out the applicable questionnaire.

There are many benefits to using the questionnaires. Some benefits are that when you overcome this particular emotion, you can look back on what you wrote and understand a little bit more of what caused this feeling, how you can prevent it or experience it again, as well as other important information that you gain by reading over the information you wrote down when you were seriously engaged in emotions.

When you are filling out the negative questionnaire, you are venting, which helps you to relax. The repeating question allows you to see if this is a problem that repeats itself or not. By filling out the questionnaire, you may realize that you need to take action if you want this problem to be solved. You are also given the opportunity to switch from how you are feeling now to how you want to feel. Finally, it allows you to realize over a period of time that no matter how bad things seem when you are filling out the form, in the end the situation was resolved and peace is achieved.

It may be in your best interest to retain the questionnaires for years so when you need to fill out something or simply look at your past, you can think about how serious the situation was to you at that time and realize how the situation was peacefully resolved, no matter how much time has elapsed.

There are also benefits for filling out the positive questionnaire. Many people will forget to fill this out when they are in a state of bliss simply because they feel they do not need any kind of help or support since they feel that everything is under control. However, it is equally as important to fill out the positive questionnaire when you are extremely happy. A benefit of completing the positive questionnaire is that you enhance your joy when you write down the details of the event. It also almost forces you to tell yourself that you can do anything that you believe you can do and focus upon! This is very important because you will become even more ecstatic when you realize all the things that you can do. It is important to note that the longer you are in this joyful state, the more positive things you will attract in your life. This is why it is crucial to walk away from anything that you feel may stir up negative emotions.

The exercises are only beneficial when you are answering the questions in detail and honestly. If you are filling out a negative questionnaire, you should feel a little bit better after filling it out, although the main benefit usually does not show until you are feeling really upset again and you look back at what you wrote. You should feel better knowing you went through rough times in the past and you will prevail.

The key to making the questionnaires work for you is detail and honestly. I have provided a few extra copies for you to utilize in the future in the back of the book. I hope you find these as effective as others and myself have found them to be.

Extreme Emotion Questionnaire (Positive)

In detail, why are you in such a great mood?

_____
_____
_____
_____
_____

What kind of things do you feel you can accomplish being in this positive state?

_____
_____
_____
_____
_____
_____
_____

What can you do to stay in this state of positive feeling?

_____
_____
_____
_____
_____

Know that the longer you stay in the state, the more positive experiences you will continue to have in the future.

Extreme Emotion Questionnaire (NEGATIVE)

What's wrong?

_____
_____
_____
_____
_____
_____

List your emotions

1_____
2_____
3_____
4_____
5_____

Is this a repeating problem?

_____

Do you *really* want to do anything it takes in order for this problem to be truly eliminated?

_____
_____
_____
_____
_____
_____

Do you believe me when I tell you that there is a positive solution that will appear sooner than you think?

_____
_____
_____
_____
_____
_____

In detail how do you want to feel right now?

_____
_____
_____
_____
_____
_____

Who do you look up to the most or have the most respect for?

_____
_____
_____

Why?

_____
_____
_____
_____
_____

What would this person tell you in relation to your current emotional/physical distress?

_____
_____
_____
_____
_____
_____

Re-read your positive emotion questionnaire you may have filled out in the book.

Read the section pertaining to your emotion in this book.

Chapter 5

The Debate

"The only thing you can't do is think that you can't do something."

— **Vincent Carotenuto**

Many people still disagree on whether it makes one happier to think of the past or the future. I have heard strong arguments on both sides. I have heard that it is better to remain in the past if it is positive, so you can relive your experiences and propel yourself to achieve greater experiences. However, I have heard stories that state you should not think of the past and just keep moving forward to achieve happiness and success and that looking back on past happy memories may cause you to become depressed and think that you can never be happy like you were before again. Both sides have valid points, however, I do not agree with either of them.

I believe you should think whatever you want if it makes you happy! If thinking back to a few years ago when you felt on top of the world makes you feel better and motivates you, do that! If thinking that you will become very successful and that motivates you, do that! Whatever it takes for you to feel good and take action to achieve your goal, do that. It really is that simple. Obviously, you don't want to just think about the past and not do anything to make yourself happy now and in the future, but reliving your past positive experiences in your mind can be comforting and healing mentally since your mind actually believes this is happening now when you really get into detail and put emotion into your thoughts. Needless to say, if you can be propelled to move forward thinking about past positive experiences, you can also be paralyzed by negative experiences that occurred in your past. I believe that this is actually amplified and is more powerful than you may realize. This is attributed to the fact that fear gripes you and can make you unable to move forward.

Right now, as I write this at 8:32 p.m. on Tuesday, April 21, 2009, pain is shooting through my jaw because of my wisdom teeth coming through. The pain has been pretty constant for a few days now, but I prevail and almost force myself to ignore the pain. When this doesn't work, I trick my brain into pretending to enjoy the constant throbs! I know I have to go to the dentist and have them extracted, but the methods I have used provide a good bit of relief. I have had bad experiences with my dentists in the past, but I do not allow this fact to paralyze me and prevent me from visiting the dentist. This is what you must do to keep growing as a person. You must learn from everything, negative and positive, that comes into your life.

I believe every single thing that happens in your life is there for you to learn from. Learn from your past and then go where you want to go with your future. I find it hard to think of this as negative events happening to you, but the thing you MUST remember is that this is temporary and this will pass. When something negative happens, most of us tend to think the worst. When we get a simple cold, some of us immediately think of the worst-case scenario. We think that we are getting the flu and will miss work and our boss will fire us even though we just won an award for perfect attendance. But in reality, you will be fine in a few days without missing work and you have worried yourself for nothing.

We humans try to brace for the worst and try to set up some sort of mental shielding that will allow us to be ready for the worst just in case the worst happens. The thing we need to keep in mind is that if something bad does indeed happen, it won't stay in the same form or have the same negative results that you are facing in the present moment. Things change daily, just like people's moods and attitudes. It is important to realize that even when you are in a state of bliss, don't expect this to last forever because this tends to delude you into a false state of euphoria. Take everything in balance. I believe the key to life is that everything changes and you must adapt to it. Remember that better things are ahead and stick with what makes you happy when you are sullen and downtrodden.

It also helps to remember that everyone has problems and everyone feels that they have the worst problems. Know that everyone is facing problems even if it doesn't appear evident. It helps to know that you are not alone.

You may wonder why I focus on how to feel better when you feel negative more than how to stay happy when you are in a good mood. This is because you lose all hope and you let go of your dreams when you are in this state of mind. It is horrible, and I don't want people to go through unnecessary pain and heartache, or I at least want to buffer the pain for you by giving you new insights. In my opinion, it does not matter whether you focus on the past as long as you are moving forward in a direction in life you want to go in.

Sometimes we all need some time to sit down, relax, and reflect on our lives. Think about what you have accomplished in life, where you are heading, what things you can change in your life to reach your goals. I believe it is vital to sit down at least twice a week and think about our past and twice a week to think about our future. Can you imagine going through life without any kind of planning at all? You wake up each morning and repeat the same actions as the day before, but expecting different results. You must change your actions if you wish to change the results that manifest in your life. When you think about your past or future, you may spend as long as you wish, as long as when you are finished with your session of thought, you leave feeling like you have benefited from the session.

Chapter 6

Perspective

"If a direct correlation with your inner emotions and your outer world experiences were established, wouldn't you pay more attention to how you are feeling?"

— Vincent Carotenuto

How can it be that one person can see a tragedy, while another person may see a miracle? It all is about perspective. How you look at things changes the whole picture around. You may have heard of stories where when someone passes away, their loved ones are naturally upset, but not paralyzed by it. They see this event in a different way to how most of us see it. They realize that even the most tragic events in life do not happen by accident, they are meant to happen and would happen regardless of what we do, say, or think. Some may still remark that an event occurred at the worst possible time or that they did not deserve this event to happen to them. I wish I could ease this person's anguish by going into the future just a few years so they can see that even though now they are crippled with fear or grief, things will settle down and that their brightest days are still ahead.

Reaching the Pinnacle of Your Emotions

If you are in any kind of emotional or physical pain, I want you to believe me when I tell you that your brightest days are ahead. This is not something I believe, it is something I *know*. I really don't care what age or set of challenges you are faced with, I tell you that your brightest days are ahead. Live by those words – when you wake up, repeat them. When you settle down to bed, let those words ease you into a deep sleep.

Those who see the glass half empty instead of half full allow themselves to believe that when something bad happens to them, their life will only be worse and worse from here on out. This is a destructive pattern of thought. Luckily, however, it is easy to change once you establish a pattern of positive thought patterns.

People can change your perspective by giving you another way of looking at something. This can be very beneficial or extremely detrimental. Say you are a dedicated worker at your place of employment. You constantly put forth an enormous amount of effort daily on a consistent basis for years. One day your co-worker tells you that management does not appreciate you and you should slow down and relax. You may not heed this advice at first. However, the next time something unfair happens to you at work, you will start questioning your own beliefs about your value in the company. As time goes on, more negative things happen to you and you slowly change your views about your job and ultimately you change your perspective and become a disgruntled employee. The opposite scenario could be substituted in this same example. This is why people can and do change perspective. We have all heard of people saying people changed ever since they were around certain types of people, well this is why. This is also why it is important to hang with people who are only going to help you in life.

While we are talking about other people and their effects on you, what I have observed is that many people are not feeling their own emotions. They are feeling for other people. If someone you admire is sad, you start to feel sad around them, even if you wouldn't be if they were happy. This is not your own emotions, it is another person's feelings. Try out this activity now; think of a situation that is bothering you. You know how you feel, but try to think of the other party as completely innocent, pretend that they do not understand that this bothers you, and in their eyes they are acting innocently. Now, doesn't this calm you down a little bit? It all depends on how you look at something. The problem didn't change, just how you thought about it did.

Chapter 7

Visualization

"Feelings can kill a man or make a man."

– Vincent Carotenuto

You can escape your current reality by visualization. The next time you are in an uncomfortable situation, I encourage you to visualize yourself in a situation of your choice. Now, I am not going to pretend that I know a lot about the Law of Attraction, however, I can sum up the entire complicated law with a brief summary: whatever thoughts you put a lot of emotion behind are the thoughts that will manifest in your present reality. So basically the thoughts that exist in your mind eventually show in the form of a physical manifestation in your life.

Now if this is your first time hearing this you are probably thinking that this is very bizarre. One of your first questions may be, "Whatever I think, will show up in my life?" Yes and no. First, can you imagine everything you think showing up in your life? That would be insane. Luckily, it is more like whatever thoughts you give emotion and focus your attention on is what will show up sooner or later in your life as long as you stay persistent in your positive thinking and put intense emotions behind your thoughts. I encourage you to read more books on the Law of Attraction and allow another author to explain in more detail this very important universal law.

Doesn't it feel good to daydream? We all have done it at one time or another. If you feel good daydreaming, I suggest you do it as often as it is appropriate. When you visualize yourself doing something you enjoy, your brain does not recognize the difference between you doing it in your mind, and you doing it in your physical body. Knowing that, this makes your visualizations even more empowering! Visualizing can be a boatload of fun.

Some people may not enjoy daydreaming only because they feel like it is no use to daydream since they can't have what they are fantasizing about. This is a bad mindset to have because you in a sense confirm to yourself that you cannot have something which is false since we can have whatever we focus on and give attention to. Yet I tell you this, the more emotion you add into your visualization, the more your adrenaline increases, and you feel like you are really living this – which in your mind you are. By you visualizing your goals, you motivate yourself and push your limits. Think of the grandest vision and realize you can have this if you believe you can and take action to obtain it. Realize that everything that exists or will exist is brought to physical existence merely with thought.

Chapter 8

In Closing

"Any problem you may have in your life you can look inside yourself to find the answer."

– Vincent Carotenuto

By now, I hope you realize that your emotions change your entire life. I hope this book has provided you with new insights and motivation to live life in a fearless, more positive way. This book is a collection of thoughts gathered over my lifetime, and I hope I have taught you something that you may not have known, or something that made you think and your life has changed for the better because of this. The attitude you put into your day-to-day routines over a period of time determine your overall attitude towards life. If you do not like how your life is going now, change your attitude. Instead of the repetitive mundane tasks you have to put up with in your life, change things around and invite in some humor. See life from the other end of the spectrum. You will be amazed at how things look when you look at other people's viewpoint on life.

We constantly learn things new all the time; you never really know when you are going to learn something that turns your life around completely. The key to handling difficult circumstances is to stay calm. If you just repeat those words in your mind when you are dealing with difficult circumstances, it will help you stay calm. Take heart knowing that someone is watching over you. Treat everyone in a respectful, loving way, no matter what that person did to you. These are all things that will help in your quest towards a satisfied, content life.

If you are a person of faith, you most likely already know that God can and does ease your blows in life. I like to think that everything that happens to me is not as painful because God softened the blow. This helps keep things in perspective for me. Thank you for reading my book and please tell loved ones about it if you feel it has helped you. I wish you much luck reaching the pinnacle of your emotions.

God Bless,

Vincent G. Carotenuto

FREQUENTLY ASKED QUESTIONS

"The past exists so you may make your future brighter."

– Vincent Carotenuto

I have complied some frequently asked questions. The reason I have included a FAQ section in this book is because it allows miscellaneous information that does not warrant a full chapter to flow. I hope these answers help clarify any questions you may still have about emotions after reading this book.

Why are you qualified to write a book about mental health with no proper credentials?

This is a great question that is very fair to ask. I believe anyone who knows anything about a topic should be allowed to do as they please with the information they have about a topic. As long as the person is doing it for the higher good and knows what they are talking about, I believe it is fine. I have studied people and the way emotions and feelings work for years now. Everything in this book is based on the way I see things. I believe this is how many other people see things also. The suggestions presented to you in this book can help improve your emotional well-being. There have been times when I have sat down and thought that I should not publish a book with no degree or title next to my name, but then I realized that the information presented will help many people, and it is worth the time to go ahead and publish the book. If you were lost, you would not distrust a person's directions to get to your destination because he was not a taxi driver, right? I believe anyone and everyone who has knowledge should express it freely. It is my strong belief that this book will help many people.

What are your goals for this book?

I started writing this book when I was eighteen. I am now nineteen years old. Many months went into this book because I wanted the information provided to be as accurate and as useful as possible. I have many goals, and believe it or not, profit is at the bottom. I would rather see people writing positive reviews on this book than have extra cash in the bank. Any profit received will go to paying for college and to charity. I would love to see this book sit on library shelves and retail shelves worldwide. This is a goal that is huge, but I will work to see it happen. I want to get the word out and allow people to realize that they should be managing their moods and not letting their moods manage them! I truly want to help people with this book, and that is the main goal I have for this book and for any other books in the future.

Do you follow your own advice regarding emotions?

I try to practice what I preach; however, as with anything worthwhile, it is a struggle at times. I would be lying if I were to say I follow everything in this book. I do try to incorporate the ideas and information presented in my daily life, and I am integrating the advice little by little in my daily life. It is getting easier for me, and it will for anyone if you put a conscious effort towards improving yourself. I think the easiest thing for me is to prolong joy. When I feel really happy, I make my day go great no matter what happens. I run off my own energy, and that is a great feeling. When I am angry, I think about what I said in my book and chuckle because not only did I say what to do, but it really works! I try to remember that no one can be happy in every aspect in their life forever. You may have a serious disease and become broke. You may be broke, but your disease may have gone away completely! This is what I mean about how no one has serenity in every aspect in their lives, no matter how it looks on the outside. The reason I am convinced that the material in the book provides emotional relief is because when I am in a negative mood, I refer to the applicable emotion and read what I said about that emotion and I feel that I calm down greatly.

How does your book compare to the many other books about emotional well-being?

Most books on mental health are written by individuals who are in their early thirties and beyond with a degree and many years of college, and they study this subject extensively. I did not; in fact, I have not attended any college classes as of yet. This may turn some people's heads the other way, while others may be intrigued to see this against-the-grain thinking and see what I have to say. Also, to my knowledge, no emotional self-improvement book is formatted the way this book is with having an 'Emotional dictionary' in the book along with other helpful information and diagrams. I wanted to separate myself from other similar books because I could have easily looked up all this information on the Internet and produced a book that way. I choose not to because I wanted to have easy to understand, easy to apply information that comes from a young mind.

Finally, mental health books that are commonplace in book stores primarily consist of jargon that most readers would not fully understand, and if they do, it is left to the reader's interpretation. My book quickly gets to the point without unnecessary fillers to make the book seem longer, and unnecessary fancy language.

What inspired you to write a book on this topic?

We all have our daily life occurrences impacted by our emotions. It may not seem like it is a big deal, but often the little things in our lives can be what upsets us and ruins our days. I wanted to write a book that could improve people's daily lives, which ultimately improves one's life in general. After applying these methods into my own life, days go by smoother and they become more peaceful than how they would go without applying the methods contained in this book. I believe that what does *not* inspire us actually *does* inspire us in a sense. Some people work extra hard so they do not live in poverty, while others keep going to accomplish a goal they have set for themselves. On days when they are tired and drained, they use the fact that they have to complete what they want to do in order to feel accomplished and keep going when the going is hard.

I love to read books. In fact, during high school, instead of eating lunch I would read business and self-improvement books.

When the last few days of school approached and our teachers would show a movie and have free days, you would find Vincent reading books on how to succeed in life. I feel that they give us so much information for the small price they cost. Some books can change people's lives forever for $16.99, don't you believe this is worth the small price tag? I hope this book does the same for you at a lower price!

What are some important messages you want to make sure your readers capitalize on?

It is important to realize that even in your darkest moments, if you look hard enough, you will find light every time – no matter what the reason is. It is imperative to remember that what you are dealing with now will *not* be as bad as it seems to you at this moment. If you truly believe this, you will bounce back from setbacks and appreciate the pleasurable moments in your life more than you would without this new mindset. Life is like a scale; you don't want to tip it too far in either direction. You don't want to become extremely depressed, but you don't want to become euphoric because in each situation when you have a setback, in the end you may feel like things are crumbling down all around you. Stay in a positive mindset, but expect setbacks as this is the way life works. Take your mistakes and learn from them. I would also like everyone to realize that most disagreements you have in your everyday life are only from a lack of understanding. Everyone has a different viewpoint and past experiences, so it is only to be expected that not everyone will see things the way you are seeing them. You may think that anybody with a brain will see a situation your way, but you must be receptive and respect other people's opinions. If you think that most of the disagreements you have had with people are only because of a lack of complete understanding, how silly does this seem to get bent out of shape about?

What are your thoughts on how to best handle hard situations?

One of the most helpful thoughts to think while enduring a tough situation is to realize that this will not last forever. If you get yourself to at least believe this alone, you suddenly see a glimmer of light in this darkness that encompasses you. This may not come easy when difficult situations occur, but it will lessen the pain. I also suggest doing any 'small thing' when you are in a depressing situation. This could be anything that brings you joy. For some this is an ice cream, for some this is a good book in front of the fire. For others this is a twelve-hour night of sleep! When you are in a down mood, you need to do things that make you happier. According to the Loops of Emotion, you will stay in a negative mood unless you change the way you think. If you are experiencing a situation that is not too serious, you may want to think about using a method I have developed called the 'Replacement Method'. This is a simple exercise that basically switches the situation you are involved in. If you are tired for example, you convince yourself that you are really full of energy. If you feel that this is a lie, you are not trying as hard as you can. You will become awake if you really convince yourself that you are not tired and are full of bubbling energy. The method works best when the situation is not urgent. Stay strong in your moment of despair, and you will prevail.

KEY TO EMOTIONAL UPLIFTING

"Offset a negative thought by creating a positive one."

– Vincent Carotenuto

I have decided to include this bonus chapter to give you a way to instantly improve your mood. Think of the most pleasant thought you can imagine. Make sure this thought feels real to you; try to feel the emotions that go along with it. If you are not feeling happy doing this, you need to think of something that seems a little bit more convincing to you. You need to really feel joyful here. Try to make this exercise as real as possible. Really get lost in this thought and lose track of time. Realize that the Law of Attraction will bring you this if you stay consistent and positive. You may not receive everything that you have envisioned all at one time, but if you are really serious and dedicated, you will slowly see things fitting in, and you will in time realize that you are on your way to your dream if you stay positive.

Pretend for a minute that you will never receive what you have thought about. Didn't it feel good to really get lost in such a perfect place? Don't you feel better now than before you started? This is what I tell many skeptics who do not believe in the Law of Attraction and most of them at least agree with me that they do feel less stressed now than they were before this activity. Remember that if you can envision it in your mind, if you work to it, you can play it out in physical form.

Extra copies of the Extreme Emotion Questionnaires
Extreme Emotion Questionnaire (Positive)

In detail, why are you in such a great mood?

_____
_____
_____
_____
_____

What kind of things do you feel you can accomplish being in this positive state?

_____
_____
_____
_____
_____

_____What can you do to stay in this state of positive feeling?

_____
_____
_____
_____
_____

Know that the longer you stay in the state, the more positive experiences you will continue to have in the future.

Extreme Emotion Questionnaire (Positive)

In detail, why are you in such a great mood?

_____
_____
_____
_____
_____
_____

What kind of things do you feel you can accomplish being in this positive state?

_____
_____
_____
_____
_____
_____
_____

What can you do to stay in this state of positive feeling?

_____
_____
_____
_____
_____
_____

Know that the longer you stay in the state, the more positive experiences you will continue to have in the future.

Extreme Emotion Questionnaire (NEGATIVE)

What's wrong?

_____
_____
_____
_____
_____
_____
_____

List your emotions

1 _____
2 _____
3 _____
4 _____
5 _____

Is this a repeating problem?

_____

Do you *really* want to do anything it takes in order for this problem to be truly eliminated?

_____
_____
_____
_____
_____
_____

Do you believe me when I tell you that there is a positive solution that will appear sooner than you think?

_____
_____
_____
_____
_____
_____

In detail how do you want to feel right now?

_____
_____
_____
_____
_____
_____

Who do you look up to the most or have the most respect for?

_____
_____

Why?

_____
_____
_____
_____

What would this person tell you in relation to your current emotional/physical distress?

_____
_____
_____
_____
_____
_____

Re-read your positive emotion questionnaire you may have filled out in the book.

Read the section pertaining to your emotion in this book.

Extreme Emotion Questionnaire (NEGATIVE)

What's wrong?

_____
_____
_____
_____
_____
_____

List your emotions

1_____
2_____
3_____
4_____
5_____

Is this a repeating problem?

_____

Do you *really* want to do anything it takes in order for this problem to be truly eliminated?

_____
_____
_____
_____
_____
_____

Do you believe me when I tell you that there is a positive solution that will appear sooner than you think?

_____
_____
_____
_____
_____
_____

In detail how do you want to feel right now?

_____
_____
_____
_____
_____
_____

Who do you look up to the most or have the most respect for?

_____
_____
_____

Why?

_____
_____
_____
_____

What would this person tell you in relation to your current emotional/physical distress?

_____
_____
_____
_____
_____
_____

Re-read your positive emotion questionnaire you may have filled out in the book.

Read the section pertaining to your emotion in this book.

www.ingramcontent.com/pod-product-compliance
Lightning Source LLC
Chambersburg PA
CBHW051712040426
42446CB00008B/842